# Holy
# Thursday

*To prepare our readers for this new edition of François Mauriac's beautiful remembrance of Jesus and His gift of Himself through the Eucharist, Mother Teresa of Calcutta offers the following meditation:*

When we look at the Cross, we know how much Jesus loved us. When we look at the Tabernacle, we know how much Jesus loves us *now*.

To give us life, He made Himself the Bread of Life. In this Sacrament of Love, Jesus continually offers long life and faithful personal friendship. To make this love more real, He gives His body to be our Bread of Life.

To be alone with Jesus in adoration and intimate union with Him is the greatest gift of love — the tender love of our Father in Heaven. The fruit of our daily adoration is that our love for Jesus is more intimate, our love for each other is more understanding, our love for the poor is more compassionate, and we have doubled the number of vocations. So let us be *all for Jesus through Mary*.

Mother Teresa, MC

François Mauriac

# Holy Thursday
## An Intimate Remembrance

SOPHIA INSTITUTE PRESS®
Manchester, New Hampshire

*Le Jeudi-Saint* was first published in 1931 in French by Ernest Flammarion Publishing Company, Paris. In 1944, Longmans, Green Publishing Company published an English translation, which was entitled *The Eucharist: The Mystery of Holy Thursday*. In 1991, with the permission of Flammarion (Paris), Sophia Institute Press® published a slightly revised hardcover edition of the Longmans, Green translation, retitled *Holy Thursday: An Intimate Remembrance*. This 1998 paperback edition by Sophia Institute Press® is an exact reprint of the 1991 edition. Quotations from Scripture are from the Douay-Confraternity translation.

Sophia Institute Press®
Box 5284, Manchester, NH 03108
1-800-888-9344
www.sophiainstitute.com

*Nihil obstat:* Arthur J. Scanlan, S.T.D., *Censor Librorum*
*Imprimatur:* Francis J. Spellman, D.D., Archbishop, New York
New York, December 14, 1943

Library of Congress Cataloging-in-Publication Data

Mauriac, François, 1885-1970
    [Jeudi-saint. English]
    Holy Thursday : an intimate remembrance / by François Mauriac ;
prefatory meditation by Mother Teresa of Calcutta.
    Translation of: Le jeudi-saint.
    Reprint. Originally published: The eucharist. New York : Longmans, Green, 1944.
    ISBN 0-918477-08-5 Cloth
    1. Maundy Thursday – Liturgy. 2. Lord's Supper – Catholic Church. 3. Lord's Supper (Liturgy)
4. Last Supper. 5. Catholic Church – Liturgy. 6. Catholic Church – Doctrines. I. Title.
BX2045.H633M3813 1989    263′ .92 – dc19    88-34643 CIP

03  04  05  06  07  08  09  10  9  8  7  6  5  4  3  2  1

# CONTENTS

Meditation on the Eucharist (Mother Teresa) . . . . . . . ii

Preface . . . . . . . . . . . . . . . . . vii

I. The Breaking of The Bread . . . . . . . . . . . . 3

II. The Epistle of Holy Thursday . . . . . . . . . . . 9

III. The Gospel of Holy Thursday . . . . . . . . . . 15

IV. The Enchantment of Holy Thursday . . . . . . . . 19

V. Holy Orders . . . . . . . . . . . . . . . 31

VI. The Stripping of the Altars . . . . . . . . . . . 39

VII. Mandatum or Washing of the Feet . . . . . . . . . 43

VIII. The Secret of Holy Thursday . . . . . . . . . . 53

IX. First Communion and Viaticum . . . . . . . . . 63

X. The Jewish Passover . . . . . . . . . . . . 71

XI. Transubstantiation . . . . . . . . . . . . 77

XII. Joy . . . . . . . . . . . . . . . . . . 87

XIII. The Blessed Sacrament and the Blessed Virgin . . . . . . 91


Biographical Note . . . . . . . . . . . . . . 99

Notes . . . . . . . . . . . . . . . . . . 101

Sources of Scriptural quotations are indicated in the Notes.

# Preface

A SIMPLE layman, a writer of novels, attempts more than he can well achieve when he undertakes to write a book about Holy Thursday.

As a poet, indeed, he could have approached such a subject without encroaching on the field of theologians and mystics. For it is enough to have received the grace of a devout childhood for the very name of this sacred day to summon up the springtimes of old. Perhaps I should have limited myself to describing the luminous mist of April over Bordeaux, the flash of the first flocks of swallows through the sky, which represented to me the bells going to Rome.[1]

---

[1] According to French legend, the bells fly away from their steeples on Holy Thursday. They gather in Rome, whence they return laden with gifts, which they scatter on their way back.

# Holy Thursday

Perhaps I should just have followed the small boy I was as far as the flower market at *La Place des Capucins*, where I used to buy a potted cineraria for the repository at the college.

It would not have been presumptuous to write pages on the anguish that welled up in me on that day: the drama of the Passion, the terror of the final examination, the wonderful vacation drawing near, the sugar candy egg I was not allowed to touch.

This Easter holiday represented perfect happiness in our eyes because, different from the vacation we had in August and September, it brought along with it neither homework nor tutor. Therefore, it resembled a perfectly delicious fruit consumed, alas, too fast: I grieved at the flight of each morning, of each afternoon.

The mysterious change of nature gave the Easter vacation a peculiar quality which alone would have made it dearer to me. After the dull winter in Bordeaux, I was enchanted by the barren, sandy ground — full of dead ferns and of living water in April. I remember those silent walks when I used to frighten the cuckoo. I would lean against a pine — the resin of which would stick to my fingers — or kneel beside a spring.

But it is not in quest of recollections of childhood that one opens a book about Holy Thursday. And perhaps my task would have been made easier had I described exactly the succession of ceremonies and explained each symbol of the liturgy.

Why did I not write that small, objective, and didactic book with which no one would have found fault?

Such a task is beyond my power.

Therefore, I followed my inclination, which was to meditate on the Eucharist, the mystery of Holy Thursday. What presumption! Legions of saints, of theologians, of doctors, of mystics, have dedicated themselves to the contemplation of this marvel. The definitions of the Councils, the revelations of the saints, the liturgical hymns, form an immense treasure to which it is foolish to aspire to add even so little.

In fact, there is nothing in the following pages that is not familiar to a child taking an advanced class in religion. If these pages were to be read only by the faithful, I would be afraid of wasting my time and theirs. But I have been thinking of the non-Christian reader, of the hostile or indifferent man who, perhaps, will thumb this little book only because my name is known to him. It is to him, first, that this book is dedicated. I shall tell him, "This is the belief of the most ordinary among the faithful. These are the feelings of one Christian among a thousand others, before the small Host. Such is the invisible God he sees, the hidden God he discerns."

This incredible mystery, which some people claim to be unthinkable, brings with itself its proof. The Eucharist is a promise which has been kept, a promise made at a definite time in history, in a certain place in the world, and attested

# Holy Thursday

by the writers of the synoptic Gospels, by St. John, St. Paul, the Acts of the Apostles and, above all, recorded in an unbroken tradition.

A promise which has been kept: this last point is connected in part at least with personal experience. Those who take part in the breaking of the bread know what they can accomplish with it and what remains, without it, beyond their strength. They know the violent, irrepressible temptation against which everything is vain but the Host.

These texts, familiar to all the faithful, elementary truths as they are, will surprise and perhaps help a few of the innumerable hearts of those who never received the word or in whom the word seemed dead. They will learn through this little book that the promise is for them, also — for them, first of all, because "the Son of Man came to seek and to save what was lost."

# Holy
# Thursday

# The Breaking of the Bread

*Le Pain que je vous propose sert aux anges d'aliment;*
*Dieu lui-même le compose de la fleur de son froment.*
*C'est ce pain si délectable que ne sert point à sa table*
*Le monde que vous suivez. Je l'offre à qui veut me suivre.*
*Approchez. Voulez-vous vivre? Prenez, mangez, et vivez.*
Jean Racine

Holy Thursday is the day when only one hour is given the Christian to rejoice in an inestimable favor: "The Lord Jesus, on the night in which He was betrayed, took bread, and giving thanks, broke it, and said, 'This is my body which shall be given up for you; do this in remembrance of me.' After He had supped, He took the chalice and said: 'This cup is the new covenant in my blood; do this as often as you drink it, in remembrance of me.'"

The anniversary of that evening when the small Host arose on a world sleeping in darkness should fill us with joy.

# Holy Thursday

But that very night was the one when the Lord Jesus was delivered up. His best friends could still taste the Bread in their mouths and they were going to abandon Him, to deny Him, to betray Him. And we also, on Holy Thursday, can still taste in our mouths this Bread that is no longer bread: we have not finished adoring this Presence in our bodies, the inconceivable humility of the Son of God, when we have to rise hastily to follow Him to the garden of agony.

We should like to tarry, to see on His shoulder the place where St. John's forehead rested, to relive in spirit this moment in the history of the world when a piece of bread was broken in deep silence, when a few words sufficed to seal the new alliance of the Creator with His creature.

Already, in the thought of the One who pronounced the words, millions of priests are bending over the chalice, millions of virgins are watching before the tabernacle. A multitude of the servants of the poor are eating the daily Bread which compensates for their daily sacrifice; and endless ranks of children, making their First Communion, open lips which have not yet lost their purity. And in the vision of the Savior, an immense multitude of unchaste persons, of murderers, of prostitutes, regain the purity of their early years through contact with that Host; it makes them again like to little children. Already on that night, He saw the pillars of Vézelay and of Chartres rising up from the midst of the land of the Gentiles, waiting for the living Bread which would give life to the world. The whole of Holy Thursday, all this long spring day, would not suffice to exhaust a meditation so resplendent with joy.

But the Mass is already finished; we must enter the darkness of the Garden — it is impossible to give joy a single minute more. For it pleased the Lord to institute the Eucharist on the very night He was betrayed. This mystery was accomplished at the very moment when His body was to be broken like the bread, when His blood was to be shed like the wine. Without doubt, it was necessary that the small Host should arise on the world at that moment, in those shadows in which the traitor had already betrayed, in which Caiphas's people were plotting their crime.

Only once during His public life had the Lord spoken openly of the marvel conceived from all eternity by His love. He remembered how much this revelation had cost Him and knew how many souls had forsaken Him that day. At the synagogue, in Capharnaum (St. John relates) had been uttered strange, scandalous words. Not only the Jews but also the disciples objected in these words: "This is a hard saying; who can listen to it?" At first they had not understood, and when Jesus had said, "The bread of God is that which comes down from Heaven and gives life to the world," they had interrupted Him, begging Him always to give them of this bread. At that moment, it seems that the Lord made so bold as to lift up a corner of the veil. "I am the bread of life. He

# Holy Thursday

who comes to me shall not hunger and he who believes in me shall never thirst." Already the furious Jews murmured against Him because He dared to say that He was the living bread — this man, Joseph's son, whose father and mother they knew.

Everything then happened as if Christ, seeing that there was no longer any reason to spare them, would deliver His secret at once and throw the inconceivable challenge to human reason. "I am the bread of life. Your fathers ate the manna in the desert and have died. This is the bread that comes down from Heaven.... If anyone eat of this bread, he shall live forever; and the bread that I will give is my flesh for the life of the world."

And as from the stupefied and divided crowd arose the question that reasonable people will keep on asking until the end of the world ("How can this man give us his flesh to eat?"), Jesus overwhelmed them with reiterated, insistent, irritating affirmations. It was necessary to shout it. The lukewarm people would leave; the timid ones would be troubled: "Amen, amen, I say to you, unless you eat the flesh of the Son of Man, and drink his blood, you shall not have life in you. He who eats my flesh and drinks my blood has life everlasting and I will raise him up on the last day."

The mystery of Holy Thursday had therefore been foretold that very day before the whole synagogue at Capharnaum. And from that moment, according to the Gospel, several disciples withdrew and they no longer followed Jesus. Being for every man the touchstone of faith and love, the Eucharist, like the Cross, divided minds as soon as it was announced.

Jesus must have seen those who withdrew, and not only these few, poor, hard-hearted Jews, but with them all those who were to be scandalized by this mystery throughout the ages. Jesus must have numbered among them the philosophers and the scientists who believe only in what they see; and the mockers, the blasphemers who, from century to century, would fight, with unrelenting animosity, the small silent Host, the defenseless Lamb.

When the renegades had withdrawn, Jesus was left alone with the twelve apostles. Then He asked them this question, and it seems that our ears can still hear His supplicating tone: "Do you also wish to go away?"

Thus, until the end of time, the Creator will plead with His creatures.

II

# The Epistle of Holy Thursday

*And they continued steadfastly in the teaching of the apostles*
*and in the communion of the breaking of the Bread.*
Acts 2:42

The eleventh chapter of the First Epistle to the Corinthians, which is read at Mass on Holy Thursday, testifies that the very day after Christ's death, His disciples believed what we believe and did what we are doing when, nineteen centuries later, we bow our heads at the moment of Consecration or when we approach the Holy Table.

Serious disorders were prevalent in the church at Corinth and the mysteries were no longer celebrated there with the required purity. St. Paul recalls incidentally to the faithful in this church what they already know: "For I myself have received from the Lord (what I also delivered to you), that the Lord Jesus, on the night in which He was betrayed...."

# Holy Thursday

There follows the account of the Last Supper, given at the beginning of this book. Then St. Paul adds, "For as often as you shall eat this bread and drink the cup, you proclaim the death of the Lord, until He comes."

Such is the sacrifice that we still celebrate. The Council of Trent taught that "the same Christ who offered Himself on the Cross, offers Himself up now through the ministry of the priests." This Flesh and this Blood, delivered for us in the elements of bread and wine, are being offered up to the Father as a bloodless holocaust. Nothing has changed since the dawn of Christianity except the order of the prayers which precede and follow the Consecration and Communion.

At the noon Masses in large parishes, the gentlemen who stand near the door of the church in the midst of an indifferent crowd, and who are waiting for the priest to finish, may not remember that what is being enacted there on the altar is exactly what was consummated in a definite moment of human history, at a place called Calvary.

But at Masses read at dawn in these same parishes or in religious communities, even an indifferent person would feel the atmosphere created by the Real Presence of the Lord on the altar, this atmosphere which makes the smallest chapel of our day resemble the catacombs. "The perpetuity of Christianity is never better felt," said Jacques Rivière, "than during these early morning Masses when a few words of prayer said aloud are heard from time to time with long intervals of silent worship by the priest — these Masses half stolen from the night."

But did St. Paul believe in this inconceivable mystery of the Real Presence which Catholics accept as an article of faith? Here is what he taught the Corinthians on this subject: "Whoever eats this bread or drinks the cup of the Lord unworthily, will be guilty of the body and the blood of the Lord...." "He who eats and drinks unworthily, without distinguishing the body, eats and drinks judgment to himself."

Not only did the first Christians believe what we believe but, furthermore, they had towards the Eucharist the same attitude which is to this day that of Catholics who alone continue to "distinguish the body of the Lord."

This explains the mysterious mingling of conflicting feelings in the man who is about to receive Holy Communion: fear and confidence, open-heartedness and remorse, shame and love. The small Host which the sinner approaches throws an impartial and terrible light on irretrievable deeds: on that which he has done, on that which he could not have refrained from doing.

No man knows himself, if he has not looked at his soul in the light of the Host lifted above the ciborium. In that moment the Church, sublimely inspired, puts on the lips of the priest and the faithful the words of the centurion: "Lord, I am not worthy that Thou shouldst come under my roof, but only say the word and my soul shall be healed" — a prayer that has always been answered since the first day when Christ heard it in Capharnaum.

All these misdeeds that the communicant sees at a glance are no longer his; someone else has taken them over since the pardon of Christ has come down on his soul with the absolution of the priest. His misery, far from driving him into despair, helps him understand how much he has been loved.

Such is the sad but precious privilege of the sinner: love had to seek for him farther, to lift him from a lower level. To take heart again, the communicant finds comfort in the fervor he himself experiences and which, perhaps, comes from God. If we love Him, it is a sign that He loves us, for it is a gift of God to love God, and He never rewards us for anything that He has not Himself given us. Thus, an almost foolish confidence overcomes all our doubts, our anxieties, and overflows the memories of the defilement of our soul. The priest, assisted by the deacon, the subdeacon, and the acolytes, is advancing toward the kneeling faithful....

Happy is he who, back at his seat after Communion, does not need any words, but adores and is silent. On the evening of Holy Thursday, the beloved apostle had rested his head on the breast of Christ; since Holy Thursday, Christ has been resting in the breasts of His friends, not only once but every morning, if they are pure of heart.

The faithful must refrain from giving too much importance to sensible favors received in Communion. Often, a person who suffers from aridity at the Holy Table will recognize suddenly the blessing of this Presence when he least expects it, during the day, when performing some task. Or else, at the moment of a violent temptation he may experience the inner certitude of not being alone, an impression of heavenly security, as if he actually heard the words: "It is I; do not be afraid." What is almost always obtained through frequent Communion is a grace which surpasses all perceptible favors; an increased light and, better still, a new strength in God.

III

# The Gospel of Holy Thursday

*Un Dieu qui, nous aimant d'une amour infinie....*
Corneille

The Gospel of Holy Thursday is taken from the thirteenth chapter of John. Jesus washes His apostles' feet. He teaches them to love one another, not by words but by example. He washes Judas's feet. He, who is aware of the abyss of agony and pain awaiting Him, kneels before those who He knows will abandon Him, deny Him, and betray Him.

He had already taught them that the Son of Man has come not to be served, but to serve. He serves them and He serves all of us in the person of these poor, worried men who cling to Him and anxiously question Him as the light of the day is slowly fading away. He disregards the objections of Simon Peter — He looks at them and says, "You are not all clean."

# Holy Thursday

He again puts on His cloak which He had taken off for the washing of the feet and returns to His seat at the table. Jesus hands Judas the piece of bread which marks out the betrayer forever. The wretched man opens the door and disappears into the darkness.

Jesus calls the eleven apostles, who no longer dare to raise their voices, "Little children." He says to them, "A new commandment I give you, that you love one another.... By this will all men know that you are my disciples, if you have love for one another." Peter asks Him, "Lord, where are You going?" And Peter assures Him that he will follow Him anywhere — he is ready to give his life.

Thus we are sometimes lifted above ourselves; we believe we can renounce everything: "I should give my life for you." From afar, it seems to be an easy task for our weak love. But how many times did the cock crow for us as it did for Simon Peter? And we did not go out and we did not weep bitterly.

Night has come, yet the only friends Jesus found in this world keep silent. He speaks to them with an immense love; He pities them — He on whom tonight no one will have mercy. He reassures them: "I will not leave you orphans." Then He unveils to them the mystery of His own life in souls, of their future union with God: "If anyone love me, he will keep my word, and my Father will love him, and we will come to him and make our abode with him" — a promise which has been kept for millions of souls through the centuries. He is the Vine, we are the branches; we live His very life. We shall love one another as He loved us. And already He announces to those who are there how much He is going to love them: "Greater love than this no one has, that one lay down his life for his friends." Thus He speaks to those who did not choose Him, but whom He chose, whom He called by their names, whom He attached to Himself, and with whom He identified Himself. (Priests should pray longer at this place.) He tells them that the world will hate them as the world hates His own Person. But let them be comforted: a joy awaits them that no one can steal from them.

At that minute, the apostles no longer doubt. Jesus looks at them and smiles, perhaps sadly, when He says to them: "Do you now believe?" He knows that the time when this faith will be shaken is drawing near. And yet what power of affirmation He reveals when He proclaims: "Take courage, I have overcome the world."

Let us go no farther; let us also plunge into darkness. Tomorrow, Friday, no Host will be consecrated; the officiating priest carries to the repository the one he reserves for that day. The altar remains empty. The *Pange Lingua* is sung until the Blessed Sacrament rests in that tomb prepared beforehand. While the Vespers are being chanted, the priest strips the altar of its ornaments. The Church enters into agony with Christ. Until the Resurrection, no bell will ring.

IV

# The Enchantment of Holy Thursday

*In days that are no more, Heaven's loving kiss in solemn Sabbath stillness on me fell; then rang prophetical, full-toned, the bell; and every prayer was fervent bliss. A sweet, uncomprehending yearning drove me to wander on through wood and lea, and while a thousand tears were burning, I felt a world arise for me. Of youth's glad sports this song foretold me, the festival of spring in happy freedom passed; now memories, with childlike feeling, hold me back from that solemn step, the last. Sound on and on, thou sweet, celestial strain! The tear wells forth, the earth has me again!*
*Faust,* Part I

I can still picture myself when I was a child, led by the hand or else riding in an old landau whose odor always revived memories of departure, baggage, train, vacation. We used to visit the repositories from the primatial Cathedral of St. André to St. Paul, from St. Paul to St. Éloi, then to St. Michel, then to Notre Dame. Perhaps I should refrain from evoking these recollections in order to follow, step by step, the liturgy of Holy Thursday. At the Cathedral, the bishop

# Holy Thursday

himself washes the feet of twelve poor men. Assisted by twelve priests, by seven deacons, and seven subdeacons, he blesses solemnly the holy oils — the oil of the sick, the oil of chrism, the oil of catechumens.[2] The oil of the sick is the matter of the Sacrament of Extreme Unction. The oil of chrism, matter of the Sacrament of Confirmation, is used also for the anointings at Baptism, the consecration of bishops, the consecration of altars, the blessing of bells, and the consecration of churches. The oil of catechumens is used for Baptism, the ordination of priests, and the consecration of kings.

But I cannot tear myself away from the repositories. I still see myself standing in my pew at the *Tenebrae* office on this sacred day, in the chapel of the college. It is my turn to chant the lamentations of the prophet Jeremias. They are a part of Good Friday's service and were formerly chanted on the night preceding that day. In the sanctuary a triangular candlestick bears as many lighted candles as there are Psalms chanted during the service, and at the end of each Psalm an altar-boy extinguishes one of the candles. This ancient liturgy has come down to us from the earliest ages of the Church: formerly, these lamentations were sung in dark churches and the candles were put out, one by one, as dawn came. But by

[2] Correctly speaking, the oils are blessed at Mass, which is in the morning. *Mandatum* follows in the afternoon, from which comes the designation *Maundy Thursday*, often used for *Holy Thursday* in old English service books. — TRANS.

instinct, I had discovered the true meaning of this symbol: each extinguished flame represented one of the apostles overcome by sleep in the night of agony. At the end, there remained only one, which was Christ — Christ burning alone in the darkness. This last candle was carried away behind the altar.

I can still hear my shrill voice and the very clear notes of one of my comrades. They rose toward the vault in unison, *"Jerusalem, Jerusalem, convertere ad Dominum Deum tuum....* All my friends have forsaken me; all those who laid snares for me have overcome me; the one I loved betrayed me...." Suddenly, from the lamentations of the prophet springs up the heartrending reproach that the Church puts in the mouth of Christ on that day: "O my vineyard that I had chosen! I had planted thee Myself: how didst thou change thy sweetness into bitterness, even as far as crucifying me and freeing Barabbas? I surrounded thee with a hedge; I took off the stones that could harm thee; and I built a tower to defend thee. How didst thou change thy sweetness into bitterness, O my vineyard...."

This grief was in me, but through the open stained-glass window I could see the beautiful blue spring sky. The plane trees in the court resounded with trills and calls. I could recognize the three notes of the soaring bird which I heard on Easter Monday in the coppice of St. Symphorien, under the trees still covered with dead leaves; and this bird, the

# Holy Thursday

warmer wind, the light, were the only perceptible signs of springtide.

In those years of innocent childhood, I began to feel in my heart two different inclinations which Holy Week helped me to realize. All the enchantments of the world were uniting against the child who wished to enter into agony with Christ. I was still indignant towards the disciples who could not watch for one hour and then, looking around, I was amused watching the aimless flutter of a butterfly driven into the chapel by the wind.

A pleasant languor, a weariness, a sweet prostration made me drag my feet in the dust as on a holiday. And the horse-chestnut trees in the squares had burst out suddenly. My pen-tray was full of beetles. At the gate of each church, numerous girls from the parish were taking up a collection for the poor. We used to play the game of giving to the prettiest or to the ugliest. We used to burst out laughing in front of them — we misbehaved, mother told us. She used to say also, "Button up your coat before entering the church; you will catch cold." Yes, I recall this sudden impression of freezing cold which pierced me to the bones under the vaults of St. André. When leaving the street flooded with light, how dark these vaults seemed to me!

The crowd was slowly passing in file before the repository. I was waiting my turn; almost nothing was left of my joy. It was vanishing, as it were, as I approached the resplendent tomb. Before reaching it, one had to press his lips against a crucifix. On a crimson-red cushion rested the image of the Savior which an altar boy wiped off with a white cloth after each kiss. Some of the faithful used to press their lips lengthily on each of the five wounds "with great affection and great grief."

It was then, perhaps, that I was the most fully sensible of the error of Protestants concerning images. The most unlettered Catholic knows that there is nothing more here than a figure, but that through the wood, his gesture of love reaches the real wounds always open, always bleeding until the consummation of the world.

The true Church does not divide man, does not treat him as a pure spirit. She appeals to all his senses, source of the greatest crimes and of the most earnest devotion; she transmutes this impure stream and turns it away from creatures; and our tears and our kisses are directed in all purity to the One who gave us this promise: "I will draw all things to myself."

On Holy Thursday, a little of the tenderness of St. Mary Magdalen warms up our frozen hearts. "Greater love than this no one has, that one lay down his life for his friends." These words of the Lord are confusedly present to the silent crowd: there He is lying on the wood, the One that the world could not convict of sin and who, nevertheless, bears the sins of the world.

# Holy Thursday

The Jews were awaiting an Alexander, a Caesar; and here is the Lamb of God, who, being spat upon, surpasses (even in the eyes of incredulous persons) all carnal and spiritual greatness. He surpasses them infinitely. Poorer than the poorest: "The foxes have dens and the birds of the air have nests; but the Son of Man has nowhere to lay his head." Betrayed by one of His people, abandoned and denied by all the others, forsaken even by God in the darkness of this Thursday; reckoned among scoundrels, given gall and vinegar to drink — perhaps it is when the Jews summon Him to come down from the Cross in order that they might believe in Him that He most confounds our pride. This silence, this acceptance of defeat, this virtual acknowledgment of defeat, disconcert us. It was necessary that He suffer all these pains, that He sink into this last desolation.

The tide which had carried me on as far as the repository was drawing me away and, once more, I was at the porch between two rows of girls who were soliciting alms. I was inhaling the smell of the asphalt pavement and of April's dust. When Easter came late in the spring, as twilight crept on, the first flocks of swifts caroled on the roofs. Happy are the Christians who recognize the imprint of God on the outside world!

Although evening was drawing near, darkness did not spread over the earth, and the earth did not quake. The tombs remained sealed over human ashes. The dead did not appear to convert the world to penance and to attest the power of the Father.

Would I consent to become a grain in the handful of salt that the Son of Man came to throw upon the earth? Would I consent to burn as the least twig of the fire that He had come to kindle? Under the straw hats the young girls' faces had grown slightly pale, their eyes somewhat tired, their mouths faintly mysterious. Would I be one of those who, blind to the beauty of the body, would look for souls, seize them, carry them to the foot of the Cross, and give them to Christ? Or would I seek for myself, would I convert my passions into a ravenous idol, demanding everything and feasting on human victims?

After my school years were over and I could leave for my vacation as early as Palm Sunday, the struggle within me became more severe in the *Landes*. At St. Symphorien the poorest inhabitants wanted to be represented at the repository, which they used to light with humble peasant lamps and copper candlesticks.... In that little village I sensed the silence of the bells much more deeply than in the city. The blacksmith's anvil, a cock, a lark, had that day a peculiar sound. I fancied the birds were not yet singing; they were only rehearsing the hymn of resurrection for the feast to be celebrated the day after the morrow.

But just the same, under the dead leaves, under the sand, and under the ashy heath, Cybele, the goddess of nature,

# Holy Thursday

began to sigh and to stretch out her benumbed arms — Cybele, more redoubtable than any of the mysterious faces one sometimes meets in the cities. Christ teaches our souls that He is the vineyard and we are the vines, but Cybele teaches a similar lesson to our bodies. Thus, the rebirth of grace and of nature were taking place in a young Christian, and between these two springtides there began a strange struggle which was to end only after many years.

Is it ever ended?

It is useless to know on which side peace is, for our miserable hearts love peace only when they are overcome by suffering. Hardly has the Lord cured them when they long to avail themselves of their renewed strength to venture again on the high seas. "The peace of God which surpasses all understanding": an incomprehensible text for young hearts ever eager for adventure, but a text that man meditates upon in his maturity without ever exhausting its substance.

The young man, hardly awakened, watches from his bed the sun of Holy Thursday bringing to life the roses painted on the curtains. Perhaps he rebels against the lesson of concentration and silence that the Church sets before him on that day. What! Enter into agony! To him, it does not seem possible that truth can be anywhere but where life is spontaneous and free: everything should burst forth, all the germs of youth in our blood.... These he does not know as yet; he does not know what he is bearing within himself. The

# The Enchantment of Holy Thursday

Spartan child laughed and pressed in his arms the young fox which was about to gnaw at his entrails. Youth, fruit that believes himself to be sound, harbors decay. Much later, as a man, when he no longer dares to look up to Heaven, he will remember the warning which had resounded in vain during the years of his innocent childhood.... And he will yearn for the bygone days when he had no misgivings upon awakening, when he ran barefoot, talked and laughed under the pine trees swaying in the blue sky of Holy Thursday.

Holy Thursdays of old, in remote country places, where the curate and a few poor women decorated a rustic repository.... Lines from Eugénie de Guérin's *Journal* preserve the memory: "I come back anointed with fragrances from the moss chapel where the sacred ciborium rests in the church. The day when God wants to repose among the flowers and the scents of spring is a beautiful day. Mimi, Rose, the sacristan, and I prepared the repository with great care. While working at it, I was thinking of the Cenacle, the well garnished room in which Jesus wanted to celebrate the Pasch with His disciples, offering Himself as the Lamb."

Eugénie's thoughts were invincibly drawn toward her beloved brother who, that spring of 1835, was wandering about in Paris, toward Maurice who, in his letters to her, no longer spoke of God and who, she feared, was about to lose his soul. "I thought of you during this ecstasy," writes Eugénie,

# Holy Thursday

"and I ardently wish you had been by my side at the Holy Table as you were three years ago.…"

On that day, many saints have seen their destiny take shape. The Cross rises up before them as it rose before their Master: all the trappings of the bloody Passion are offered to them. Let us listen to the Little Flower, Thérèse of the Child Jesus: "Not having obtained permission to watch at the Altar of Repose throughout Thursday night, I returned to my cell at midnight. Scarcely had I laid my head on the pillow when I felt a hot stream rise to my lips, and thinking I was going to die, my heart almost broke with joy. I had already put out our lamp, so I mortified my curiosity till morning and went peacefully to sleep."[3]

What stoic was ever capable of such a mortification? Was it blood? Her very life was at stake. However, the wise virgin did not light her lamp but remained peacefully in the darkness of Holy Thursday. The little girl awoke at dawn, trembling, perhaps, because of what she was going to learn. "At five o'clock, the time for rising, I remembered immediately that I had some good news to learn, and going to the window I found, as I had expected, that my handkerchief was saturated with blood. What hope filled my heart! I was firmly convinced that on the anniversary of His death my Beloved had

---

[3] Thomas N. Taylor, *St. Thérèse of Lisieux, the Little Flower of Jesus* (New York: P.J. Kenedy & Sons, 1927), 154.

allowed me to hear His first call, like a sweet distant murmur, heralding His joyful approach...."

Thus, on Holy Thursday, it is sometimes made known to souls, and even to the most ordinary, that agony and death must not be feared but awaited and desired. From the moment that Christ entered His agony, men received the promise that they would no longer go through the shadow of death alone.

V

# Holy Orders

*The priest in whom the sacred character conceals the human aspect
disturbs by his mere presence the dark and secret things that lurk within us.
The earth trembles under the foot of Jesus Christ.
The ferret has been put into the warren....*
Paul Claudel

The Eucharist must not prevent us from considering the other sacrament which was instituted on Holy Thursday: Holy Orders. "Do this in remembrance of me." "Do this, as often as you drink [the cup], in remembrance of me."

The twelve apostles are the first twelve priests; Judas is the first bad priest. They were themselves so keenly conscious of being no longer men like others that their first task, after Jesus had disappeared from their sight, was to replace the traitor, Judas: "Therefore, of these men who have been in our company all the time that the Lord Jesus moved among us, from John's baptism until the day that He was taken up from us,

# Holy Thursday

of these one must become a witness with us of His resurrection." "And the lot fell upon Matthias, and he was numbered with the eleven apostles."

Now they are ordained, the first members of an innumerable family. Holiness entered the world with Christ. The Church is holy and what matters to us the wretchedness of individuals, their falls, their betrayals? "The great glory of the Church," writes Jacques Maritain, "is to be holy with sinning members." Until the end of the world, the hands of a few chosen men will never cease to lift up "the Lamb of God who takes away the sin of the world." It was through the imposition of hands that even in those early days Stephen was made deacon — Stephen whose face, as it is recorded in the Acts, appeared to the Sanhedrin "as though it were the face of an angel." That light which shone on the face of Stephen has never been extinguished through the ages; and, in spite of all denials, it has never ceased to bathe the faces of lowly priests; it shone on the humble visage of the Curé d'Ars.

The grace of Holy Thursday will be transmitted unto the end of time, unto the last of the priests who will celebrate the last Mass in a shattered universe. Holy Thursday created these men; a mark was stamped on them; a sign was given to them. They are like to us and yet so different — a fact never more surprising than in this pagan age. People say that there is a scarcity of priests. In truth, what an adorable mystery it is that there still are any priests. They no longer have any human advantage. Celibacy, solitude, hatred very often, derision and, above all, the indifference of a world in which there seems to be no longer room for them — such is the portion they have chosen. They have no apparent power; their task sometimes seems to be centered about material things, identifying them, in the eyes of the masses, with the staffs of town halls and of funeral parlors. A pagan atmosphere prevails all around them. The people would laugh at their virtue if they believed in it, but they do not. They are spied upon. A thousand voices accuse those who fall. As for the others, the greater number, no one is surprised to see them toiling without any sort of recognition, without appreciable salary, bending over the bodies of the dying or ambling about the parish schoolyards.

Who can describe the solitude of the priest in the country, in the midst of peasants so often indifferent, if not hostile, to the spirit of Christ? We enter a village church; we find only an old priest kneeling in the sanctuary, keeping a solitary watch with his Master. The words of Christ concerning priests are proven every day: "I am sending you forth like sheep in the midst of wolves.... You will be hated by all for my name's sake." For centuries, since the first Holy Thursday, some men have chosen to become objects of hatred, without expecting any human consolation. They have chosen to lose their lives because once Someone made them the seemingly foolish promise: "He who finds his life will lose it, and he who loses his life for my sake will find it." And elsewhere: "Every-one who acknowledges me before men, I also will acknowl-edge him before my Father in Heaven."

But if they did not find their joy even in this world, would they persevere? "What are you going to do?" said Abbé Perreyve to Christ, the day before he was ordained. "You are delivering Yourself; You are abandoning Yourself to me. You surrender Your Body to me. I shall use it for my needs and for the needs of other souls.... I shall touch You, I shall carry You, I shall handle You and You will allow me to do it; I shall place You on the lips of whom I will; You will never refuse...." In-deed, priests, holy priests, are repaid by an immense love.

For every Christian who tries to live according to his be-lief, inevitable scandals count for little when one considers the holiness of the Catholic priesthood as a whole. Let the heretics boast of not needing anyone to reach God. Do they believe that worthy Catholics do not enjoy the delight of sol-itude in contemplation and union with the Father? But it is because of its conformity with our fallen nature, with our wounded nature, that Catholicism shows itself to be the true Church. Only in her bosom is kept the promise that Christ made to His disciples, on that Thursday: "I will not leave you orphans." From the very beginning of His public life, He had testified to the power given to the Son of Man to forgive sins. And this power was transmitted to His priests: "Whose sins you shall forgive, they are forgiven them."

Protestants see in the Sacrament of Penance a means of easy forgiveness, but only so that one may sin again. One is helpless against such a distorted notion. Let us not cease to repeat to them that, in order that absolution be valid, one must first *hate* one's sin, a prerequisite which, in certain cases, is very difficult to achieve. Next, we must resolve never to sin again — and this is not only a matter of words but an inner determination of which God is the only judge. Last, the fear of punishment does not suffice if it is not inspired by love of God. No one can be forgiven without a beginning of love.

Through the visible priest, the invisible Christ forgives our sins and opens again His heart to us. That is why those faithful who are eager to make some progress in the spiritual life not only confess but agree that a priest direct them in this difficult path: "I will not leave you orphans." Spiritual paternity, which the world deems hateful, is nevertheless the token of salvation. Even if it requires a great effort for human pride to submit to it, its fruits are admirable. No action in the world gives us, to the same degree as does this voluntary subjection, the certainty of our own freedom. This light yoke, to which we are not compelled to submit, we must desire, we must accept, through an act of free will unceasingly renewed. The faithful subject themselves in order not to be slaves. They submit in order to remain free.

It will be objected that, nevertheless, the faithful suffer from it; that saints themselves have suffered from it; that direction was for some a source of great distress, and even that they sometimes found in it an obstacle much more than an efficient aid; and, on the other hand, that some souls were able outside of Catholicism to reach a high degree of perfection without any such help.

But perhaps those souls lacked precisely this resemblance with the Christ of Holy Thursday, obedient even unto death: this last defeat which consummates the Christian's victory. The submission of the penitent to his spiritual director puts it within the power of the most humble of the faithful to make that complete renunciation which is demanded for the slightest progress in the following of Christ.

Furthermore, there does not exist any other means of looking at oneself full in the face; for it is not with our own eyes that we can see ourselves: "If thou knewest thy sins," said Christ to Pascal, "thou wouldst lose courage." No one can judge oneself impartially; we have to know ourselves, but at the same time we must not lose courage. It is this balance that the faithful Catholic obtains from spiritual direction. Those who are reckless lose exaggerated confidence in themselves; those who are timid are reassured, and, at last, they understand fully the words spoken by St. John: "If our heart blames us, God is greater than our heart."

No, it is not to a man that we submit, but to Jesus Christ whose place he takes. And it is admirable to know how the most common priest, as soon as he has put on the stole and lifted his hand above our bent heads, is stripped of his own personality, is changed for us into another person who is infinitely greater than himself. Besides, this man, this priest, is himself submitted to another priest. The Pope is penitent and is directed. The man before whom we kneel, kneels in his turn — he who judges is judged. He hears our sins but he confesses his own. Confession, penance, contrition, constitute the sacred patrimony shared by all priests and all the faithful.

We receive three inestimable treasures: *the certainty of being forgiven* through the words of Jesus to the paralytic, repeated expressly for us: "Thy sins are forgiven"; *a kiss of peace* received in the very depths of our miserable hearts; *a blank page* upon which the most infamous man, having become once more like a little child, can begin writing his life anew...for it is never too late to become a saint.

Such is the immense stream of grace which has its source in the first priestly ordination of this sacred Thursday.

# VI

# The Stripping of the Altars

*Blood covered our nakedness....*
St. Catherine of Siena

After the short Vespers of Holy Thursday, the officiating priests strip the altar of all ornaments and recite meanwhile the twenty-first Psalm with the choir. It is the Psalm of which the first verse was cried out by the dying Christ: "O God, my God…why hast Thou forsaken me?"

The evangelists did not falter before this apparent acknowledgment of defeat, and no doubt it was necessary that the chalice be drunk to the dregs, even to this total abandonment. At that minute, nothing but vanquished humanity appeared any longer in Christ.

How could the Son of God have believed Himself to be forsaken? Had He not known and accepted His martyrdom beforehand? He knew it, without doubt, and He also knew that everything that was happening in that moment had been prophesied in that very twenty-first Psalm, the first verse of which He was crying out to His Father.

None of the scribes, who at the foot of the Cross were shaking their heads and scoffing at the dying victim, thought of drawing a parallel between the desperate appeal which opens this Psalm and what follows: "All they that saw me have laughed me to scorn; they have spoken with the lips and wagged the head. He hoped in the Lord, let Him deliver him: let Him save him, seeing He delighteth in him."

But then was it not precisely the same mockery which the chief priests and rulers had just used against Jesus crucified? Were they not laughing at Him because, having saved others, He could not save Himself? Were they not challenging Him to come down from the Cross because He said He was the Son of God?

But, above all, they who knew the Scriptures should have remembered verses seventeen through nineteen, which were being confirmed at that very moment in an astonishing manner: "They have pierced my hands and feet. They have numbered all my bones." "They parted my garments amongst them and upon my vesture they cast lots."

And this twenty-first Psalm, which begins with a cry of doubt and distress, ends with the promise of a triumph that the Crucified alone was to achieve. "All the ends of the earth shall remember and shall be converted to the Lord; and all the kindred of the Gentiles shall adore in His sight. For the Kingdom is the Lord's; and He shall have dominion over the nations."

# VII

## Mandatum or Washing of the Feet

*We know that we have passed from death to life,
because we love the brethren....*
1 John 3:14

After the stripping of the altars, the ceremony called *Mandatum* takes place. It is named after the first word of the antiphon: "*Mandatum novum do vobis.* A new commandment I give you." The Gospel is sung: "*Ante diem festum Paschae.* — Before the feast of the Passover." Then, the officiating priest divests himself of the cope, girds himself with a cloth, and begins the washing of the feet of twelve clerics or of twelve poor men. He kneels in front of each one, washes, wipes, and kisses the foot held out to him, using the cloth that the deacon offers him.

Each verse which is chanted during the ceremony of the washing of the feet affirms the new law which is to change the world, the law of love, unknown to antiquity: "By this will all men know that you are my disciples, if you have love for one another." And furthermore: "So there abide faith, hope, and charity, these three; but the greatest of these is charity." And finally: "Where charity and love are, God is there also."

By the washing of the feet, repeated each Holy Thursday, through the insistent words which make clear its significance, the Church bears witness that she is conscious of the love that pervaded the world on that day, love that it is her mission to keep alive and to spread abroad.

Nothing is less congenial than this love to the nature of man. Since Holy Thursday, the charity of Christ has been making its way painfully against human cruelty. Men used it for selfish purposes, even when they pretended to adopt it. Love for the lowly served as a pretext for atrocious slaughters, for unbending tyranny. Love flourishes only in Christ. The world accuses the faithful of not doing anything except out of self-interest and with the hope of future rewards; it is because the world is blind to the nature of that love which is the source of the superhuman devotion of which the Catholic Church presents innumerable examples. To love Christ, particularly in the Eucharist, and to love one's neighbor, are one and the same thing; the two commandments are blended with one another: "Amen, I say to you, as long as you did it for one of these, the least of my brethren, you did it for me." It is not a question of calculating, or anticipating the reward in advance — it is a question of love.

In the words spoken by Christ first to His disciples, then to His Father, on the night between Thursday and Friday, were contained all those words of love that would be directed to Him by generations of saints. In the same manner, the washing of the feet prefigured all those works of charity which would change the face of the world. During this holy night, a likeness is created forever between other suffering bodies and the suffering body of the Son of God. Two families will spring up among the friends of Christ — first, the men and women who will dedicate themselves directly to the alleviation of His sorrowful humanity, those who will partake of His agony; then, the men and women who will serve Him in the suffering bodies of the poor, the crippled, the imprisoned, the plague-stricken, and all the outcasts of the human race.

The first family, composed of those who are called *contemplatives*, scandalizes the world which does not suspect the exhausting activity of its members. The world cannot understand a life entirely consumed in meditation upon Christ's sufferings.

A few lines taken from *La Vie mystique d'un Monastère de Dominicaines au moyen âge*, by Jeanne Ancelet-Hustache, may enlighten the world in that respect. We read there that one of the nuns "believed that she saw our Lord while He was being maltreated by the Jews. This vision overwhelmed her

# Holy Thursday

with such a grief that, henceforth, she could no longer sleep. In the evening, after Compline, she retired, but even before all the nuns had gone to bed, she was up again and she remained praying in the dormitory until choir time. After Matins she remained in the choir. In winter, when it was very cold, she threw a blanket over herself, but never left the choir. Only once she went to bed but, at Prime, she believed she saw before her Our Lord, who told her: 'At this hour, I was standing in front of the tribunal; you are lying down and sleeping.' "

Foolishness, St. Paul himself calls it. Truly, it is a folly of love that Holy Thursday spreads in the world, but it meets with an opposition that will end only with the world. Paganism, apparently conquered (and even at that, only in one part of the planet), survives in its lowest forms in every living heart. But it is, above all, limited natural reason which struggles against the fire that Christ came to light during the night between Thursday and Friday. Such reason fights against Him with all its might. Even at the height of Christendom there were great thinkers who, denying original sin, accepted and trusted human nature alone — those who had confidence in man as he is, who sought for balance and measure in everything, who did not want to give up anything of themselves and whose ideal was self-fulfillment.

Wise people, exasperated at the mystics, call out for help: "Brothers," begs Nietzsche, "remain faithful to earth with all the strength of your love. Let your love and your knowledge be bent to earth. I beg you, I pray you. Do not allow your power to fly away from terrestrial things and to beat its wings against eternal walls. Alas, so much energy was always lost! Imitate me, bring back to earth this wasted energy; indeed, bring it back to flesh and life."

One cannot deny the strength of this reproof. But, it is powerless against the faith of those who know that the flesh is corrupt and that life is not Life. If their wings keep on beating against the eternal wall of which Nietzsche speaks, it is because they know of a door in the wall, a narrow door which allows light to enter and through which they themselves can slip in.

The pagan appeal of Zoroaster has been overcome ever since that night between Thursday and Friday when Christ uttered this priestly prayer: "I in them," said He to His Father, speaking of His disciples, "and Thou in me; that they may be perfected in unity, and that the world may know that Thou hast sent me, and that Thou hast loved them even as Thou hast loved me."

The whole human race has, as it were, been lifted up by this leaven of folly. During those periods when reason was worshipped, there always remained one voice to bear witness that this folly continued.

In this practical and matter-of-fact century, a humble little girl who died in 1897 suffices to attest to the persistence of this folly. A child of the bourgeoisie in Lisieux rises to the same heights as Catherine of Siena or John of the Cross.

"O Eternal Word! O my Savior!" the Little Flower, Thérèse of the Child Jesus, said to Christ, "Thou art the Divine Eagle whom I love and who allurest me. Thou who, descending to this land of exile, didst will to suffer and to die, in order to bear away each single soul and plunge it into the very heart of the Blessed Trinity — Love's eternal Home! ...Forgive me, O Jesus, if I tell Thee that Thy Love reacheth even unto madness, and at the sight of such folly what wilt Thou but that my own heart should leap up to Thee?...

"I know well that for Thy sake the Saints have made themselves foolish; being 'eagles' they have done great things. Too little for such mighty deeds, my folly lies in the hope that Thy Love accepts me as a victim.... O my Divine Eagle! As long as Thou willest I shall remain with my gaze fixed upon Thee, for I long to be fascinated...."[4]

Thus, the wise men and the fools gaze upon one another from afar and, even in their dispute, they have no understanding of one another. None of their arguments is of any value to the adversary. The worshippers of the Sacred Heart claim that they rely on the reasons of the heart which reason ignores. "The heart has its order, the mind has its." To Pilate who asks Him "What is truth?" Christ does not give any

---

[4] Taylor, St. *Thérèse of Lisieux*, 207-8.

answer. The state official, the serious and important man, could not understand.

But between the two kinds of minds, there was always a group of hesitating people, of men in agreement with both systems of reasoning. During His life Christ met them: those who first had followed Him, then had withdrawn, shocked, scandalized by His unreasonable words referring to the Bread of Life which is His flesh. Really, that went beyond all limits; that was not believable. They did not wish to be taken for fools.

Then there were the shrewd and prudent people, like Nicodemus, who came to Jesus by night in order not to be seen — like Joseph of Arimathea, a disciple of the Savior, "although for fear of the Jews, a secret one." Their hearts were touched but their minds were unyielding. They were over-prudent people who drew back from anything that might seem foolish.

Since then, even among the avowed followers of Christ there have always been a great number who consider the worldly spirit with complacency, with eager complicity; all those who follow Him, but from a distance and without taking upon themselves the weight of the Cross; all those who pray to Him but in secret, and who are so incapable of any folly of the Cross that they turn the Cross to their own material advantage, thus playing their game as skillfully as those in the opposing camp.

# Holy Thursday

Let us recognize that ambitious Christians of this kind content themselves with weakness, fear, and cowardice, with all those things that Nietzsche denounces in slaves; and sometimes they do this more successfully than worldly people. They are less hindered by these defects: they know a way of "glorying in their misery" which the Apostle had not foreseen and it is that which gives a good opportunity to the adversary. The adversary triumphs and points the finger of condemnation at them, whilst referring to the words of Christ concerning the estimate of the Christian tree by its fruits: their fair outward appearance but interior decay, which is worse than rotten fruit. But he is wrong when he triumphs: there is only one name for the good fruit of the Tree — it is holiness. What about the rest of the fruit? The rest is what was lost and what will nevertheless be saved because God is Love.

But the saints exist. They are innumerable, most of them are unknown, except those whose mission it is to enlighten the world. Why more than to another is this privilege granted to a young tubercular Carmelite in a cloister in Lisieux? Why, soon after her death, did grace flow out from her cell and cover all the earth? Why is she invoked throughout the whole world? Living saints exist, we know it — unknown saints like the Curé d'Ars, in whom no one, perhaps, will ever know that they see Christ face to face, held in their trembling hands. For one Curé d'Ars, for one Thérèse de Lisieux, whose tombs are thronged by crowds, thousands of saints live, suffer, and die unknown.

The adversary does not see these multitudes of saints, or he turns his eyes away from them. He disregards their merits and their virtues and refuses to see their holiness, trying instead to throw the spotlight on false Christians. There, he has an easy task playing havoc. However, neither mediocrity nor meanness of soul is the prerogative of any one party. But the same mediocre being who does not shock anyone in the world becomes offensive to us if he makes use of the Cross. Anywhere but on Calvary he would remain unnoticed. It is the enormous disproportion between such an opportunist and the truth which he claims to profess which makes the task so easy to a Nietzsche or to Bernanos, the magnificent but unjust author of *La Grande Peur des Bien Pensants*.

# VIII

# The Secret of Holy Thursday

*God, consider that we do not understand ourselves, and that we do not know what we want, and that we swerve infinitely from what we wish.*

*Oh, how difficult it is to make this understood by hearts which do not know by experience how sweet is the Lord.*
St. Thérèse

The image of the mustard seed, the smallest of all seeds, which grows into a large tree where the birds of heaven build their nests, can be applied to this mystery manifested during the night between Thursday and Friday.

Twelve frightened men who feel that death is hovering near crowd around the Son of Man whose hand is lifted over a piece of bread and over a cup. Of what value is this gesture, of what use can it be? How futile it seems when already a mob is arming itself with clubs, when in a few hours Jesus will be delivered to the courts, ranked among scoundrels, tortured,

# Holy Thursday

disfigured, laughed at by His enemies, pitiable to those who love Him, and shown to be powerless before all. However, this Man condemned to death does not offer any defense; He does nothing but bless the bread and the wine and, with eyes raised, pronounce a few words.

It seems that, after nineteen centuries of extraordinary glorification, the small Host for which so many cathedrals have sprung up, the small Host that has rested in millions of breasts and that has found a tabernacle and worshippers even in the desert — it seems that the triumphant Host of Lourdes and of the Eucharistic Congresses of Chicago and Carthage remains as unknown, as secret as when it appeared for the first time in a room in Jerusalem. Light is in the world as in the days of St. John the Baptist, and the world does not know it.

The debates of philosophers, the disputes of statesmen always lead to religious questions. The point in question is always God and those who believe in Him. An ambitious person must never pronounce the name of Christ if he does not wish, because of this name, to be hated by all. There where the Prince of this world triumphs, the only obstacle that must be destroyed is Christ. He remains the last stone to obstruct the path of triumphant man, master of matter and of souls and of all the forces of life. He remains this stumbling block, this stone which, even when it is overturned, is still the cornerstone.

# The Secret of Holy Thursday

But even those who speak of this stumbling block with most hatred and fear do not know anything about it. They are almost as puzzled by this enigma as the chief priests and rulers who ravaged the first little Galilean church. The secret of Holy Thursday is spread over the whole world, but nevertheless it remains impenetrable to those outside. One must be *of it*; one must be incorporated *in it*; one must be part of the vine; one must be among the branches.

Why do young girls accept the ascetic life of Carmelites, of Poor Clares? Why do strong young men choose a scorned black robe, the sign of chastity and of renunciation? What motivates them? Why do men and women suddenly stop in the midst of a dissipated life and turn from their evil ways? And those who used to enjoy nothing but uncleanness become anxious to be pure in every one of their thoughts. Sometimes even their faces, their looks, their laughter change.

More astonishing still, if the old temptation arises again — if concupiscence which they believed to be dead springs up once more and seeks to possess them — they are strong to resist. Such sins which contemporary authors of pagan philosophy and psychology declare inevitable, become by a strange inversion what those regenerated souls can no longer do, even when flesh and blood urge and insist.

What do they have in them, those who victoriously resist or who rise again as soon as they have fallen; those who

# Holy Thursday

hasten to wash off the slightest stain; those who can no longer bear to be impure? The monotony of repeated rites, the routine, the daily weariness which proceeds from habitual acts — none of these have the effect which one might logically expect.

The faithful may sometimes feel happy when they realize that this secret is incommunicable, but more often they experience anxiety. There are said in Paris certain Masses during which the priest, the acolytes, the faithful in the nave, and the nuns behind the grilles feel united. Indeed, they do not partake equally of love and graces; but between the most holy and the most unworthy there prevails, as it were, a pre-established harmony, a concert orchestrated by the Spirit, a miraculous symphony into which a non-believer cannot penetrate.

Mystery of joy! We shall be able to persuade you of what is evident to us only after you have entered. Do you believe it impossible to escape this circle? No, for it is for you to seek the light. God disposes the hearts of those who search for Him. He who seeks Him, finds Him. The door opens to him who knocks. But how many refuse to search for light, look purposely in the wrong direction, and willfully divert their thoughts from the quest of truth!

O mystery of Holy Thursday, defenseless as love is ever defenseless! O mystery, ever prepared to deliver itself, to unfold itself, to be enclosed again in each soul which even half-heartedly welcomes it! Only to human indifference does it remain impenetrable.

The secret of Holy Thursday was borne by Christ during three years of His mortal life. He was a man like us — of flesh and blood — but, as God, was conscious of His destiny and knew the path He had to walk.

As soon as He had performed His first miracle at Cana, He doubtless had present in His heart the secret of the Eucharist. He could change water into wine. He performed this miracle before all. The water became wine; the wine would become blood. From afar, He was preparing the minds of men while He disposed their hearts.

How difficult it would have been to tell this secret if He were not God! Not only did the bread and wine become His flesh and blood, but it was necessary that this food be distributed to all those who were hungry and thirsty; it must never be lacking, in order that all might be fed. The two multiplications of bread, performed one after the other, attested again to the omnipotence of Christ. The bread having been multiplied, He would dare at last to pronounce the first words referring to the mystery of Holy Thursday.

Jesus bore the burden of His secret, but each time He confided in His friends they were scandalized: they did not understand. Nothing in the Gospel is more moving than those confidences which seem to be almost involuntary, those brief hints of what He was preparing. Sometimes Christ stopped speaking after the first words as if the silence of His friends had discouraged Him, as if their questions, their slowness to comprehend, kept Him from proceeding any farther.

Nothing is more spontaneous than these words which, as it were, escaped Him, words whose vibration rings down the ages and which showed, as in a flash of lightning, the Cross already prepared to receive Him. For example, the answer to John's disciples, who were scandalized because the disciples of Jesus were not fasting: "Can the wedding guests mourn as long as the bridegroom is with them? But the days will come when the bridegroom shall be taken away from them, and then they will fast."

And when at last He unveiled the Passion in precise terms, the disciples were irritated.... What loneliness the living Christ knew then!

It is not when He withdrew into the desert that He felt the greatest loneliness, but when He was in the midst of the flock of those wavering hearts which the Spirit had not yet kindled. Doubtless, it was necessary that the man in Him be reassured by the God so that He would not lose heart when confronted by the infinite disproportion between His message and the poor human race destined to receive it.

However, He did not dedicate Himself to solitude as have so many men of genius. He did not flee from the crowd, but gave Himself up to it. What gives Christ as a man a unique character among the masters of the world is first this gift of Himself, this complete abandonment of Himself to the crowd. Before being delivered, He delivered Himself. He does not belong to Himself, not having come to be served, but to serve. He is the slave of slaves. Nothing belongs to Him. He lives in the street, in the fields, in villages. Miserable bodies affected with leprosy crowd Him, suffocate Him. He seeks refuge in a fishing boat, in order to be able to breathe. Dirty hands grab His cloak; virtue springs from Him.

No one kept less aloof; no one was ever less guarded, more accessible — such He is still today in the tabernacle, given up entirely to all — yet nevertheless, He was alone with His Father, in that mysterious, ineffable union which He sometimes confessed, for this secret also escaped Him: "No one knows who the Father is, except the Son."

He stood alone, without any other witness but Himself of what was accomplished in His sacred person. Because of His purity He remained isolated in the midst of the crowd.

"Which of you can convict me of sin?" It is by their passions that men know that they belong to the same race. They all slip in the same direction; they roll down the same slope. How strange this man (who is in their midst and who does not sin) must appear to them! The greatest saints speak of sin as of a death through which they have passed or, at least, a death that they could have suffered and that threatens them until the end. But Jesus is unaffected by the inclination of the flesh and knows nothing more about sin than the punishment linked to it. Not being able to commit sin, He atones for it.

Are these the speculations of theologians? No. Everything that was accomplished had been announced literally by Isaias:

> And he shall grow up as a tender plant before him and as a root out of a thirsty ground; there is no beauty in him, nor comeliness: and we have seen him and there was no sightliness that we should be desirous of him:
>
> Despised and the most abject of men, a man of sorrows and acquainted with infirmity; and his look was, as it were, hidden and despised, whereupon we esteemed him not.
>
> Surely he hath borne our infirmities and carried our sorrows; and we have thought him, as it were, a leper and as one struck by God and afflicted.
>
> But he was wounded for our iniquities, he was bruised for our sins; the chastisement of our peace was upon him and by his bruises we are healed.
>
> All we like sheep have gone astray, every one hath turned aside into his own way; and the Lord hath laid on him the iniquity of us all.
>
> He was offered because it was his own will and he opened not his mouth; he shall be led as a sheep to the slaughter and shall be dumb as a lamb before his shearer.

# The Secret of Holy Thursday

*By his knowledge shall this my just servant justify many and he shall bear their iniquities.*

*Therefore, will I distribute to him very many and he shall divide the spoils of the strong because he hath delivered his soul unto death and was reputed with the wicked; and he hath borne the sins of many.*

# IX

# First Communion and Viaticum

*At last there dawned the most beautiful day of all the days of my life. How perfectly I remember even the smallest details of those sacred hours! The joyful awakening, the reverent and tender embraces of my mistresses and older companions, the room filled with white frocks, like so many snowflakes, where each child was dressed in turn....*
St. Thérèse

*Lord, I shall see you no more with the eyes of the flesh....*
St. John of the Cross (dying, to the Host which had been brought to him)

But human indifference is unfathomable; this explains Christ's loneliness in the sacrament of Holy Thursday. It also explains man's blindness as it is expressed in the significance many attach to "First Communion."

Some may be touched by these celebrations which, on a Thursday in spring, fill the streets with little brides and with young boys clamped in their first starched collars. Actually,

# Holy Thursday

however, in many families, especially those of the working classes, the occasion of First Communion does not begin anything, but ends everything. It testifies that the child is henceforth freed from church and priest. Now, the serious things in life can be considered.

The most beautiful day in life! This formality perpetuates among us the betrayal by a kiss: how many children receive Christ only as a signal that they are giving Him up. It is a sign officially recognized by all, which means that they are going to abandon Him.

However, on that day some privileged souls seal a pact with the forsaken God: many religious vocations spring up in the grace of First Communion. The Little Flower recalled the sweetness of this "first kiss." For her, as for many more ordinary children, it was not the kiss of Judas, but the beginning of an alliance never to be broken. "Our meeting could no longer be called a simple glance," she writes, "but a fusion. We were no longer two. Thérèse had disappeared like a drop of water in the midst of the ocean. Only Jesus remained...."

In spite of this, even in a Christian country, those truly faithful to the Eucharist represent only a handful of the people. Devout but despised *fauna* of weekday Masses — old women, old men, with irritating foibles — you amongst whom the bad Christian is ashamed to kneel, but behind whom the truly faithful wishes to hide his misery: you are the only true, intimate friends of Christ! Sometimes I perceive your eyes fastened on the small Host and I see in them the look of the centurion which has come down to us through the centuries. I recognize the prostration of the Canaanite, the joyous haste of Zaccheus, the attentive love of Mary Magdalen. Always the same ones are there, the same disdained and timid group which, sometimes scattered, always gathers again. They are the faithful whose faith was never taken away and who, before and after Communion, repeat instinctively the same words which were pronounced at the dawn of Christian history — words endowed with such power that they gain instead of lose force with time, so that they suffice to split open a brazen sky and to bring down, at once, a warm rain on the barren heart of a man: "My Lord and my God!"

May the grace be granted to us not to die without the *Viaticum*,[5] to enter the mystery of death with the only Friend who can pass over its threshold with us. May we be granted the grace to meet again beyond the dark regions the One who so humbled Himself as to unite His flesh, His blood, and His divinity to a body already corrupt and more than half-destroyed. May He hear our imperceptible sob, the last, that no one else in this world will be able to hear. May He receive on His adorable face our last breath which will not even tarnish

[5] Communion received by a person in imminent danger of death.

# Holy Thursday

the mirror pressed to our lips. May we go to sleep with Christ, may we be buried in the Eucharist, to awake at the feet of Christ the King, conqueror of the world. And may He be blessed in our immense hope not to die alone.

Cowardice? Fear of death? It is easy to discredit that hope with one word. If there are men who are so engrossed by the thought of death that they fail to live, there are others to whom death teaches the meaning of life. Is it because we are courageous that we do not dare to look death in the face? Courage consists, on the contrary, in pondering upon death and in seeking instruction from that inevitable teacher. Even outside the faith, that meditation is the foundation of all greatness. Let us recall what the great men of ancient times owe to the contemplation of death and, in modern times, the attitude of a Montaigne, a Goethe, a Proust. These men throw the light of death on ebbing life, on disintegrating humanity. The thought of death enriched their knowledge of man. Before death struck them down, they themselves had time to steal a few human secrets from it.

For us, turning toward "this gate opening on the unknown heaven," our attention is much less drawn by those things that death lights up in this world than by the source from which they come. The thought of death would be vain and even fearsome had it no other object but to be used in psychological investigation and to develop in us an attitude of stoical detachment or hedonistic frenzy. But upon the redoubtable threshold, to our joy there stands the slender form of "that little girl, Hope," as Péguy describes the second virtue. Like the young martyrs who concealed the Holy Species from the executioners, she presses in her frail arms the ciborium where a last Host is waiting for us.

Such is the refuge that Love prepared for us on the night between Thursday and Friday. But let us guard against seeing it only as an inn where the table is set and where God awaits and dwells with us despite the lateness of the hour. All this, indeed, it is; and this is the aspect under which it should first be shown to disheartened souls. As Jacques Rivière says: "We must act as if someone were looking everywhere without seeing what is being pointed out to him; we should place our hand upon his shoulder and say, 'But look! Here it is, right here.' "

However, let us not assume the blasphemous attitude of certain writers who have presumed to speak of the Host as a sedative or an anesthetic. This place on high where you seek and find rest for your souls is not a quiet place. Love is never perfectly calm. Nothing engages a man as much as does the Eucharist.

"Build your houses on the rim of Mount Vesuvius," declared Nietzsche, meaning that it is necessary to live dangerously. The man who partakes in the breaking of bread dares to build his house in the very core of love. He becomes, as it were, Godlike, but regardless of the strength he derives from it, his free will remains. We are always free to disown this immense grace, to abuse it. The greatest love may be betrayed. Fed on the living Bread, we nevertheless conceal a part of ourselves which longs for swine's food.

The Eucharist engages us unreservedly; it is a pact of love, an alliance signed in the deeper recesses of our being. All our potentialities are called upon to warrant the protection and fulfillment of this pact. But betrayal can be appraised only in terms of this alliance and this pact.

Christ warns us that we must answer for what we have received. When it is Himself we have received, what shall we not have to answer for?

"You are clean, but not all." That word, pronounced during the night of Holy Thursday, extends beyond the narrow circle of the friends of Christ where only Judas's soul was stained. What pardoned sinner kneeling at the Holy Table does not sometimes ask himself if he is not about to eat and drink to his own condemnation?

Those who denounce Christian weakness and Christian cowardice cannot even imagine the boldness that the repentant sinner needs when, standing among the faithful as they approach the Holy Table, he sees the moment of Communion draw near. Happy are those who, in that moment, can so immolate themselves that they no longer see themselves. And hardly indeed has He, who out of love conceived the Eucharist, crossed the threshold of a miserable, loving but terrified heart, but He casts all fear away. He brings His peace with Him, according to the promise made to us on Holy Thursday. The slightest movement of love is sufficient to restore courage and confidence in the soul.

But do not believe that Communion is an easy gesture, a meaningless routine, or even a mere consolation, an emotion, a certain manner of closing one's eyes, of resting one's head in one's hands.

The essential mistake of Nietzsche is not to have understood that supreme love cannot exist without supreme daring, and that the man who proceeds forward, hands clasped, toward the small Host, risks everything and beholds, sometimes heroically, his whole life as at the hour of death. And he overcomes this horror. As he proceeds forward, he plunges into an infinite adventure. The passionate life which Nietzsche places so high, the "purple life," is experienced by the faithful Christian in that moment to a far greater degree than by the Caesar Borgias and all the weak, enslaved brutes whose example is put before us by Zoroaster.

Jacques Rivière says: "No other religion ever used love as an intermediary between the faithful and his God; love with its tremendous disturbances, with its extravagant logic, with the confusion it puts in the soul." One should add, "love, with its flashing light, with the self-knowledge which suddenly awakens the soul and keeps it, as it were, standing on watch, on guard — love which compels one to

# Holy Thursday

remain armed, always ready, because the Bridegroom is at the door."

Holy Thursday's mystery of love gives strength to the weak, daring to cowards, freedom to slaves, nobility to vile individuals, purity to the debased, mercy to the implacable. To all, it unveils both the wretchedness of human pride and the tremendous power of heroic humility.

X

# The Jewish Passover

*He is mediator of a superior covenant enacted on the basis*
*of superior promises. For had the first been faultless,*
*place would not of course be sought for a second.*
Hebrews 8:6-7

*Now, in saying a 'new covenant' He has made obsolete the former one; and*
*that which is obsolete and has grown old is near its end.*
Hebrews 8:13

At the end of this meditation on Holy Thursday, it remains
for us to give the reader desirous of going farther in his knowledge of the Holy Eucharist, if not a complete outline of
dogma, at least some directions for his search.

When we consider any action of Christ, we must always
remember that according to His own words, He did not come
to destroy the Law but to fulfill it. The Eucharist must not
be considered as a marvelous improvisation. In reality, this
marvel was deeply rooted in the Jewish Law. The Jewish

# Holy Thursday

Passover (*la Pâque juive*) prefigured the Christian Easter (*la Pâque chrétienne*)[6] and for centuries the paschal lamb symbolized the Lamb of God. As it is said in the *Office for the Feast of Corpus Christi*, "The Bread of heaven puts an end to symbols."

"I have greatly desired to eat this passover with you." Therefore, it was from the legal Passover of the Jews (*la Pâque juive*) that the new Easter (*la Pâque chrétienne*) was born. Passover (*la Pâque*) means "passage," because that celebration commemorated the exit of the Jews from Egypt and their coming into the promised land. In the same manner, the Christian Easter transfers us from a sinful state to a state of grace, from darkness to light, from the flesh to the spirit, from death to life.

God, speaking through the mouths of Moses and Aaron, had given this order to His enslaved people:

*On the tenth day of this month let every man take a lamb by their families and houses. But if the number be less than may suffice to eat the lamb, he shall take unto him his neighbor that joineth to his house, according to the number of souls which may be enough to eat the lamb. And it shall be a lamb without blemish, a male of one year.... And you shall keep it until the fourteenth day of this month; and the whole*

---

[6] As can be seen, the French language signifies the close relation between Passover and Easter by employing the same word for each: *la Pâque*. Unfortunately, translation obliterates many of the connotations arising from the author's use of this one term for both feasts. — TRANS.

*multitude of the children of Israel shall sacrifice it in the eve-*
*ning. And they shall take of the blood thereof and put it upon*
*both the side posts and on the upper door posts of the houses*
*wherein they shall eat it. And they shall eat the flesh that*
*night roasted at the fire, and unleavened bread with wild let-*
*tuce. You shall not eat thereof anything raw nor boiled in*
*water but only roasted at the fire. You shall eat the head with*
*the feet and the entrails thereof. Neither shall there remain*
*anything of it until morning. If there be anything left, you*
*shall burn it with fire. And thus you shall eat it: you shall*
*gird your reins and you shall have shoes on your feet, hold-*
*ing staves in your hands, and you shall eat in haste; for it is*
*the Phase (that is, the Passage) of the Lord.*

So, a share of the lamb is offered to God and the other share is eaten by the people. The two essential features of the Eucharistic sacrifice are thereby prefigured. In the new Easter (*la Pâque chrétienne*), as in the ancient Passover (*la Pâque juive*), the victim is at once a holocaust for God and food for men.

The altar is a table as well. Commenting on the words: "Take ye and eat, this is my body which shall be delivered for you…," Bossuet adds, "The body of the Lord is truly eaten as it was truly delivered up; it is as truly present on the table where it is consumed as it was on the Cross where it was deliv-ered unto death, where it was voluntarily offered, bled to death for the love of men."

# Holy Thursday

One of the commands that God gave to Moses and Aaron was that they should use unleavened bread for the Passover celebration. Although under the new law it is not necessary that the Eucharistic bread be unleavened, the external aspect of the Host, according to the usage of the Roman Church, is the same as that of the ritual bread prescribed by the ancient law. Thus, during the centuries spent in expectation of Christ, the Host was represented on the tables of the chosen people.

The blood of the paschal lamb was to be "put on both the side posts and on the upper door posts" in order that the death-dealing angel would recognize the houses of those who were to be spared. In the same way, the blood of Jesus Christ is put upon us: after we have received Communion, the gate of our heart is dripping with that blood which wards off the evil spirit.

Here, we no longer have an image but an invisible reality experienced by any faithful soul. That same temptation, that same roaring lion against which yesterday we were as helpless as a prey already captive and resigned, may be still lurking around us. It is still lying in wait; but our heart, protected by the Body and Blood of Christ, is armed against its assaults. Communion carries an adequate power that each one can verify in himself — a power at which we shall never cease to marvel. It is the flame in the darkness that the traveler kindles to drive away wild beasts.

# The Jewish Passover

The ancient Passover was instituted when the Hebrews were in Egypt, anticipating a deliverance to come. The new Pasch was instituted by the living Christ. He had at His disposal His flesh still untouched, His blood which had not yet been shed.

The Jews celebrated the Passover in the memory of their deliverance. The Eucharistic sacrifice is also primarily the memorial of the death of the Lord: "Do this in memory of me." But the Jews could only eat the paschal lamb once a year; we may receive it every morning, if we are pure of heart.

# XI

# Transubstantiation

*We celebrate the memory of the last Pasch of Christ, and of that night when He wished to share with His brothers the lamb and the unleavened bread, according to the instructions given to their forefathers. After the figurative lamb, the meal being finished, we confess that the Body of the Lord was given with His own hands to the disciples, entirely to all and entirely to each.*
St. Thomas Aquinas

The faithful Catholic who communicates receives the entire person of Christ: body, blood, soul, humanity, divinity. Let us try to contemplate this mystery.

We have seen that the mystery of Transubstantiation is based on the affirmation: "This is my body, this is my blood." Bossuet aptly remarks that when Christ uses comparisons, symbols, or similes, the evangelists always make it clear. But here, the Lord speaks with the same authority as when He says "Thy sins are forgiven" or "Arise and walk."

# Holy Thursday

"O Lord," says Bossuet, "how clear, how precise, how strong, how powerful are your words. Hardly are the words pronounced: 'Woman, you are cured' — and she is cured immediately. 'This is my body' — and it is His body. 'This is my blood' — and it is His blood.

"Who can speak in that manner if not the One who holds everything in His hand? Who can be trusted if not the One for whom doing and speaking are one and the same thing? My soul, accept these words without reservation: believe as firmly as the Lord spoke. Believe with as much humility as He shows authority and power. The Lord wants to find in your faith the same simplicity which He put in His words."

Luther, who destroyed and denied so many things, submitted to these words; he did not try to rebel against their divine simplicity. Zwingli's exegesis, according to which "this is" would be the equivalent of "this is the symbol of," exasperated him, and he defended the Eucharistic presence with his usual rudeness.

At the Marfurt conference, where the landgrave of Hesse had introduced Luther to the Swiss theologians Zwingli and Oecolampadius, in order that they might achieve doctrinal unity in Protestantism, Luther wrote on his desk with chalk, "This is my body," and he remained unshaken in his belief.

However, he, too, diverged from the Catholic belief on an essential point concerning the Eucharist. To Luther, the glorified and omnipresent body of Christ was bound, joined, closely united with the bread and wine, but was not substituted for them. Furthermore, the Real Presence was not the result of the words pronounced by the officiating priest. In the Catholic Mass, at the solemn moment of Consecration, Jesus retains the effective power, but the priest is united to Him as an instrument in the hands of God. The divine power works through the priest the miracle of the Transubstantiation of the bread and wine into the Body and Blood of Christ.

According to Luther, the substance of the Body and Blood of Christ is merely *associated with* that of bread and wine; according to the Catholic Church, the substance of the bread and wine is *changed into* the Body and Blood of Jesus Christ. The *accidents* of the bread and wine (exterior appearance, color, taste) do not change, but the *substance* is transformed and becomes really the Body and Blood of Jesus Christ.

In the inspired stanzas of his hymn *Adoro Te*, St.Thomas Aquinas sings:

> *O Godhead hid, devoutly I adore Thee,*
> *Who truly art within the forms before me.*
> *To Thee my heart I bow with bended knee,*
> *As failing quite in contemplating Thee.*
>
> *Sight, touch, and taste in Thee are each deceived;*
> *The ear alone most safely is believed.*
> *I believe all the Son of God has spoken.*
> *Than Truth's own word there is no truer token.*

# Holy Thursday

*God only on the Cross lay hid from view,*
*But here lies hid at once the manhood, too.*
*And I, in both professing my belief,*
*Make the same prayer as the repentant thief.*

*Thy wounds, as Thomas saw, I do not see.*
*Yet Thee confess my Lord and God to be.*
*Make me believe Thee ever more and more;*
*In Thee my hope, in Thee my love to store.*

*O Thou memorial of Our Lord's own dying!*
*O living Bread, to mortals life supplying!*
*Make Thou my soul henceforth on Thee to live:*
*Ever a taste of heavenly sweetness give.*

Does the dogma of the Eucharist depend upon scholastic distinctions of substance and form? The author of this small treatise would not presume to deal with these questions, but on that subject, he highly recommends a book, easy to read and of moderate length, by Jacques Maritain, called *The Angelic Doctor*.[7]

We learn through this book that no *human* philosophy can claim to be Catholic philosophy. Inasmuch as it is a human doctrine, Thomism is not a dogma, for any truth which became a dogma was already contained in revelation. Such a truth should not be identified with language,

[7] Jacques Maritain, *The Angelic Doctor: The Life and Thought of St. Thomas Aquinas*, trans. J.F. Scanlan (New York: Longmans, Green & Co., 1931).

with formulas — be it even the language, the formulas of Thomas Aquinas.

But the pressing, almost imperious invitation of the Church must be enough for the faithful to have recourse to the writings of the Angelic Doctor, who is also the Doctor of the Eucharist. No one has ever better defined the Holy Eucharist, and that is the reason that no one has ever written more beautiful prayers to it. The definitions of Thomas Aquinas burst forth in inspired and illuminating verses such as the *Lauda Sion*, the *Pange Lingua*, the *Sacris Solemniis*, and other hymns of the admirable *Office of the Blessed Sacrament*.

Other testimony in favor of Thomas Aquinas fully agrees with that of the Church: it is the testimony of Christ Himself. "At Paris," Jacques Maritain relates, "when the masters sought his advice as to the proper method of teaching the mystery of the Eucharist, he first went and laid his answer on the altar, imploring the crucifix. Brethren who were watching suddenly saw Christ standing in front of him on the draft which he had written and they heard these words: 'Thou hast written well concerning the Sacrament of my Body and thou hast well and truthfully resolved the problem which has been put to thee, so far as it is possible to be known on earth and described in human words.' "[8]

How admirable is the faith of Thomas Aquinas in the Real Presence! But may we rightly speak of faith in a man who

[8] Maritain, *The Angelic Doctor*, 56

sees, who knows, who contemplates? Let us gather his last words of adoration to the Body of the Lord which the priest offered him in the *Viaticum:* "I receive Thee, Price of my Redemption, *Viaticum* of my pilgrimage, for love of whom I have studied and kept vigil, toiled, preached, and taught. Never have I said aught against Thee; if I have done so, it was through ignorance and I do not persist in my intention, and if I have done anything ill, I leave the whole to the correction of the Roman Church. In that obedience I depart from this life."

In the eyes of the dying St. Thomas, the Eucharist appeared as the essential reality. The Eucharist is what is most real in the world. This is why one must accept It without reservation. He who once pronounces this acceptance with his whole heart and his whole spirit will no longer find in the Host a stumbling block to faith but, on the contrary, the very food of that faith. He who once pronounces this acceptance will no longer be able to keep away from Communion (whereas formerly he may have been unable to refrain from committing sin). When tormented by doubt, by anguish, by troubles of the soul and of the flesh, in the midst of the worst perturbations of mind and soul, he will be saved as long as he remains worthy to sit at the banquet prepared to alleviate his miseries.

It is not when everything seems to be lost that one must forsake the Host; on the contrary, it is when all seems lost and if the state of grace is maintained or recovered, that one must feed on the Host and rely on the solemn and reiterated promises of the Lord. The Eucharist never deceived those who remained faithful to It through all vicissitudes; Christ is never the first to leave us.

Let us rejoice that we were born in an age when no doctrine of mistrust or fear concerning frequent Communion prevails. Let us thank God for having prompted His Church earnestly to invite us to receive Christ as often as we can.

And since so few people now hear the words, "Come to me, all you who labor and are burdened," let each of us, when he approaches the Holy Table, look upon himself as the delegate of all those he loves or has loved, living or dead. When God makes His way into our souls, He does not find us alone. All those from whom we proceed and who have gone to sleep before us may receive, in Purgatory, some benefit of the grace pervading us, their living children, when we pray for them. And all our friends who are kept away from the Source of grace by sin, indifference, ignorance, and incredulity — those who have helped us and those we have harmed — are present in our thoughts in this ineffable instant.

With still more reason, the Host unites us with our brothers in Christ: "Because the Bread is one," says St. Paul, "we, though many, are one body, all of us who partake of the one Bread."

# Holy Thursday

The bond created by the breaking of Bread is deeply felt by all those artists and writers who live separate from their fellowmen — prisoners of their studio, of their books, or of their work. They claim their places in the human procession leading to the Holy Table. They become once more a unit in the flock. They are linked to all the others; they are no longer the limbs separated from the body. "When I give way to the kindness of my heart," said Christ to St. Gertrude, "when I humble Myself in the sacrament of life to be united to a soul which is free from mortal sin, all those who dwell in heaven, on earth, and in Purgatory receive inestimable favors."

At the moment of receiving Communion, anxiety disappears. The terrifying subtleties concerning predestination are carried away by an inner feeling that God is love. Then, the trembling soul hears the words of the risen Christ, "It is I; do not be afraid." Thus my patron saint, Francis de Sales, while experiencing one day the deepest agony, received from Christ this unforgettable solace: "I am not called He *who condemns;* my name is Jesus."

But it is especially on Holy Thursday that disturbed hearts must recover confidence and believe in the love that God has for them. One Holy Thursday, at Lauds, while the antiphon *"Oblatus est quia ipse voluit"* was being chanted, the Lord said to St. Gertrude: "If thou believest that I was willingly offered on the Cross, do firmly believe that I still wish to offer myself up each day for any sinner as lovingly as I sacrificed myself for the salvation of the whole world. That is why any man, although he feels overwhelmed by the burden of his crimes, must hope for pardon through the offering of my Passion and death. For there does not exist on earth any more efficient remedy against sin than the loving memory of my Passion."

# XII

# Joy

*O my God and my Creator, Thou piercest us with the darts of Thy love*
*and Thou leavest the shaft in the wound, and the wound is invisible.*
*Thou killest us and yet Thou leavest us more alive.*
St. Thérèse

If it is true that the communicant must neither give too much
importance to perceptible graces nor be deeply affected by an
apparent barrenness of the soul, nevertheless he must welcome joy with simplicity of heart when it is given to him. Joy
must be received as the token of the love which knows our
weakness and which has compassion on our hearts. In the
*Office of Corpus Christi*, the antiphon of First Vespers praises
this extreme sweetness of the Living Bread; thence, we can
enjoy it safely and peacefully. How entrancing is the accent
of the Benedictine nuns when they sing this antiphon: "How
sweet, O Lord, is Thy spirit, who, to show Thy sweetness to

# Holy Thursday

Thy sons, sends them from heaven a most sweet Bread, filling the hungry with good things...."

This same delight is presented by St. Thomas Aquinas (in the postcommunion of the same feast) as the prefiguration of eternal happiness. In fact, the promise made to us by Christ is renewed by each Communion. We who are eating this Bread shall not die. As the sheep of His fold, we are being marked out each time more deeply by the Good Shepherd for salvation. We are holding in our hands the token of our victory over evil in our militant life, the token of our everlasting triumph. He who is our food on earth will be our reward in Heaven, and that food is already a foretaste of heavenly bliss.

In an antiphon of the *Office of the Feast of Corpus Christi*, "*O sacrum convivium*" (the very antiphon that the priest recites while bringing back the Sacred Species to the tabernacle after giving Communion outside of Mass), St. Thomas summarizes in a few words the different aspects of the Eucharistic mystery: "O sacred banquet, in which Christ is received, the memory of His Passion is renewed, the mind is filled with grace, and a pledge of future glory is given to us...."

That the Infinite Being may humble Himself to the point of disappearing under the appearance of bread and wine, that the purity of God may be united to a corrupt flesh, transcends understanding. But to those who humble their minds before this mystery, a light is always given; faith is fortified by the very trial which was meant to test it.

This God who, as the psalmist said, built His tabernacle in the sun, now establishes Himself in the very core of the flesh and the blood. This ineffable union is nevertheless accomplished, and not only with the most holy souls but with the humblest sinners, when they are forgiven. Thus the foolish demand of human desire is at once purified and satisfied. "When enraptured by human love," writes Bossuet, "who does not know that men consume themselves, that they waste themselves, that they wish they could mingle and embody their own substance in the very substance of the loved one? As the poet said, they wish they could ravish even with their teeth what they love — in order to possess it, to feed on it, to unite with it, to live by it."

XIII

# The Blessed Sacrament
# and the Blessed Virgin

*During that agony of Jesus, I saw the Holy Virgin overwhelmed
with sorrow and anguish, in the house of Mary, mother of Mark....
She fainted several times, for she saw distinctly several phases of the
agony of Jesus. She had already sent messengers for news,
but, unable to wait for their return, she went, full of anxiety,
with Magdalen and Salomé as far as the valley of Josaphat. She was
wearing a veil and as she proceeded, she would often stretch her arms
toward the Mount of Olives, because she saw in spirit Jesus
bathed in a sweat of blood, and it seemed as if she were trying
to wipe the face of her Son with her outstretched hands.
I witnessed the soaring of her soul toward Jesus who
thought of her and who cast a glance at her as if looking for help....*
Anne Catherine Emmerich

St. Francis of Assisi loved France because the sacred Host was
more venerated there than in any other country in the world.
It is remarkable that in spite of the spread of worldliness and
irreligion, the Eucharist has been more and more glorified

# Holy Thursday

and honored from century to century. The Eucharistic life of Christ has developed in the world as did His human life on earth. Jesus began to breathe in the seclusion of an obscure workshop and rose gradually to infinite glory. Likewise, the first Christians fed on the Bread of Life, but they did so in darkness.

But even when It is hidden, the Host gives life to the humblest church. Neither hymns nor lights are necessary to let us know that It is there. The small lamp only attests Its presence. The temples of those who deny the Real Presence are like corpses. The Lord was taken away and we do not know where they have laid Him. We can feel the gloominess of those churches, and especially of those which were formerly Catholic. Now, they resemble tombs sealed upon nothingness. A Catholic church remains always open, like the Heart forever open.

*Corpus Christi*.... This body of Christ was brought forth by the Blessed Virgin, and this is why the veneration paid to the Virgin Mary goes hand in hand with the cult of the Eucharist — without rivaling it and, *a fortiori*, without rising above it. But we do not separate the Mother from the Son.

Lourdes, where non-Catholics imagine that we accord Mary undue eminence, is no doubt that place in the world where Christ in the Eucharist is most glorified. It is the only place in the world where, under the veil of the Host, Christ mingles in the midst of so many rich people and is as closely pressed by them as He was during His mortal life. His mother prays for these bodies and these souls, and Christ cures them. The procession of the Blessed Sacrament in Lourdes starts from the Grotto to show that Jesus was given to us by the Virgin. And she who stood on Golgotha, at the foot of the Cross of the condemned Man, stands here by the side of the King of eternal glory.

On that Holy Thursday night, where did the Blessed Virgin take refuge? Did she know what was coming? Did she know that the time had come for her to suffer the blow she had been expecting for so many years? She was away from her Son because it was necessary that she be absent. Had the Mother been with Him, the Son would not have experienced complete abandonment; hardly would He have felt Judas's betrayal. If His Mother had been there, she would have followed her Son to the Garden; she would have watched with Him, and He would not have suffered from the desertion of His friends. He would no longer have been left alone to bear the sins of the world. She would have wiped the bloody sweat from her Son's brow. The cup would not have been drunk to the dregs.

The Virgin Mother does not appear in the drama of Calvary until her crucified Son, lifted up between heaven and earth, can no longer receive any help from her. Perhaps the

# Holy Thursday

feet were nailed low enough so that she could press her lips against them? Conversely, we learn that the day after the Ascension of our Lord she was seated in the Cenacle with the Apostles. The new disciples were persevering "in the communion of the breaking of the bread and in the prayers."

The faithful console themselves over the sorrows of the Blessed Virgin when meditating on the unfathomable joy that the Eucharist must have given her. The Virgin Mary is the only Mother who was granted the privilege of bearing her Son a second time. Who then dared to draw this parallel between the presence of Christ in the Virgin's bosom and His presence in the heart of the faithful communicant? St. Gertrude, about to receive the Host, asked, "O Lord, what gift are you going to grant me?" And Jesus Himself answered, "The gift of my whole being with my divine nature, as formerly my Virgin Mother received it."

The Lord's Supper, to which the Virgin leads us in order that we may partake of her joy, is renewed every morning. The table is always set, the Bread always offered. The Christian makes his way to eternity from Communion to Communion. At each stage in the journey, Christ is waiting for him in order that he may renew his strength and take heart again.

But let us take care not to allow too much time to elapse between these stages. Long before the grace of a Communion has grown weak in us, long before the silence and peace which emanate from a Communion have been dispelled by nature and the world, we must make our way into the radiant sphere of another Communion. Let there be no opportunity between two Communions for a period of darkness in which we would run the risk of falling into snares. We have nothing to fear if Christ marks out our life. Hardly have we had time to lose Him when already we have found Him again.

A contemporary pagan poet speaks of this God with whom no excess is forbidden. How difficult it is to abuse Communion! The only requisite to sit down at that table is the nuptial garment, that is to say, the state of grace and love.

But the Eucharistic life shapes our lives even in the world. Everything matters; every idle thought, every diversion that we indulge in diminishes our ability to receive Communion. We learn from personal experience that after attending a party where we committed no other sin but to dissipate our energies, we no longer dare to approach the Holy Table. How significant this word *dissipation* is here. We have dissipated a treasure. Our very being, re-created by the Eucharist, has been imperceptibly diminished and corrupted by the world. Sometimes the devout soul, uneasy and dissatisfied with himself, examines his conscience and does not find anything definite to be censured. Yet he knows he has lost something.

The Eucharist confers on any life an atmosphere of its own. For those who do not live sheltered by a cloister, the struggle is circumscribed between the peaceful silence of the

# Holy Thursday

Eucharist and the agitation, the gossip, the laughter of life. According to the rule of St. Benedict, the monks should refrain from talking too much. They should not indulge in idle talk or in conversation which leads only to laughter; they should refrain from laughing immoderately.

This rule, which has value for religious, has value for simple laymen as well. The Eucharist obliges the faithful in the world to build for themselves an inner cathedral, a mysterious cathedral hidden in the depths of the soul. Whenever we converse at social gatherings, glittering with sophistication and vivacity, we may not realize it then, but we find out when we are alone again: *we have drifted away*. How much ground we have lost! We must retrace our steps; we must travel again the whole length of the road.

During our thanksgiving after Communion, every idle word we say, every frivolous agitation we consent to, interposes itself between us and Christ. We build with our own hands a wall which separates us from Him. Christ is no longer near us; His word reaches us from a greater distance. But such is His mercifulness that our slightest impulse of humility and repentance suffices to overcome each barrier.

Just as the world makes us gradually men of the world, so, too, frequent Communion refashions our souls. The Eagle hollows out in our being a nest commodious for Himself. He impresses therein the shape He loves to repose in: the shape of His own body. Thus shaped — or rather transformed — our heart will conform itself less and less to the demands of outward things. But, irresolute as he may be, will not he who has known the ardent silence of the Eucharist conclude by leaving to God...the final word?

# Biographical Note

## François Mauriac (1885–1970)

From his earliest days, François Mauriac's Catholic faith permeated his sensibility and served as the dominant force in all aspects of his life and work. Born in 1885 in Bordeaux, France, and educated there in Roman Catholic schools and at Bordeaux University, Mauriac gained instant fame from his early novel, *A Kiss for the Leper* (1922).

In more than 30 books and in countless articles and essays, Mauriac took as his constant theme the glory and dignity of man, particularly as revealed in fallen man's struggle against evil and his yearning for God.

He was elected a member of the French Academy in 1933. During World War II he used his political writings to serve

# Holy Thursday

the French Resistance; after the war, he became a brilliant editorial writer for *Le Figaro*.

In both his fiction and non-fiction works, Mauriac saw man's interior spiritual struggle as a drama in which each of us must wrestle with the vicissitudes of our faith and the temptations of this world. Although his emphasis on the darkness of sin and man's struggle against it has led some to consider Mauriac's writings pessimistic, at the very heart of each of his works is a keen awareness of the overpowering reality of God's love and of man's ability to transcend his limitations with the aid of God's grace.

In 1952, Mauriac won the Nobel Prize for Literature "for the deep spiritual insight and the artistic intensity with which he has in his novels penetrated the drama of human life." As the Nobel Presentation Address rightly indicated, "François Mauriac remains unequalled in conciseness and expressive force of language; his prose can in a few suggestive lines shed light on the most complex and difficult things."

When François Mauriac died in 1970, Time Magazine reported that he "provided his own eulogy in a recording he made to be released after his death: 'I believe,' he said, 'as I did as a child, that life has meaning, direction, and value; that no suffering is lost; that every tear and each drop of blood counts; and that the secret of the world is to be found in St. John's "*Deus caritas est*" — "God is Love." ' "

# Notes

Preface

"The Son of Man came to seek...." Luke 19:10

## I. The Breaking of the Bread

*"Le Pain que...."* "The Bread I offer you is the food of angels; / God himself makes it from the purest white flour. / This delicious Bread does not appear on the table / Of the worldly people you follow. I offer it to those who wish to follow me. / Draw near — Do you long for life? Take, eat, and live."

"The Lord Jesus, on the night...." 1 Cor. 11:23-26

"This is a hard saying...." John 6:62

"The bread of God...." John 6:33

"I am the bread of life. He who...." John 6:35

"I am the bread of life. Your fathers...." John 6:48, 52

"How can this man...?" John 6:53

"Amen, amen, I say...." John 6:54, 56

"Do you also wish...?" John 6:68

# Holy Thursday

## II. The Epistle of Holy Thursday

"For I myself have...." 1 Cor. 11:23
"For as often as...." 1 Cor. 11:26
"Whoever eats this bread...." 1 Cor. 11:27
"He who eats and drinks...." 1 Cor. 11:29
"Lord, I am not worthy...." Matt. 8:8 (paraphrase)
"It is I...." Luke 24:36

## III. The Gospel of Holy Thursday

*"Un Dieu qui...."* "A God who loves us with an infinite love...."
"You are not...." John 13:11
"Little children...." John 13:33
"A new commandment...." John 13:34, 35
"Lord, where are...." John 13:36
"I will not...." John 14:18
"If anyone love...." John 14:23
"Greater love than this...." John 15:13
"Do you now believe?" John 16:31
"Take courage...." John 16:33

## IV. The Enchantment of Holy Thursday

"Jerusalem, Jerusalem...." Resp., Lesson 1, Good Friday at Matins
"O my vineyard...." Jer. 2:21; Resp. and Ver., Lesson 3, Good Friday at Matins
"I will draw...." John 12:32
"Greater love than this...." John 15:13
"The foxes have dens...." Matt. 8:20
"The peace of God...." Phil. 4:7

## V. Holy Orders

"Do this in remembrance...." Luke 22:19
"Do this, as often as...." 1 Cor. 11:25
"Therefore, of these men who...." Acts 1:21, 22
"And the lot fell upon...." Acts 1:26
"The Lamb of God who...." John 1:29
"As though it were...." Acts 6:15
"I am sending you forth...." Matt. 10:16, 22
"He who finds his life...." Matt. 10:39
"Everyone who acknowledges me...." Matt. 10:32
"I will not leave you orphans." John 14:18
"Whose sins you shall forgive...." John 20:23
"If our heart...." 1 John 3:20
"Thy sins are forgiven...." Matt. 9:5

## VI. The Stripping of the Altars

"O God, my God...." Ps. 21:2
"All they that saw me...." Ps. 21:8, 9
"They have pierced...." Ps. 21:17, 18
"They parted...." Ps. 21:19
"All the ends of the earth...." Ps. 21:28, 29

## VII. *Mandatum* or Washing of the Feet

"*Mandatum novum do vobis*...." John 13:34
"*Ante diem festum Paschae*...." John 13:1
"By this will all men know...." John 13:35
"So there abide faith...." 1 Cor. 13:13
"Amen, I say to you...." Matt. 25:40

# Holy Thursday

"I in them...." John 17:23
"What is truth?" John 18:38
"Although for fear...." John 19:38

VIII. The Secret of Holy Thursday

"Can the wedding guests mourn...." Matt. 9:15
"No one knows who...." Luke 10:22
"Which of you can convict me...." John 8:46
"And he shall grow up...." Isa. 53:2-7
"By his knowledge...." Isa. 53:11-12

IX. First Communion and *Viaticum*

"My Lord and...." Acts 20:28
"You are clean...." John 13:10

X. The Jewish Passover

"I have greatly desired...." Luke 22:15
"On the tenth day...." Exod. 12:3-11

XI. Transubstantiation

"Thy sins are forgiven...." Matt. 9:2
"Arise and walk." Matt. 9:5
"Come to me...." Matt. 11:28
"Because the Bread is one...." 1 Cor. 10:17
"It is I...." Luke 24:36

XIII. The Blessed Sacrament and the Blessed Virgin

"In the communion...." Acts 1:14; 2:42

# Sophia Institute Press®

Sophia Institute® is a nonprofit institution that seeks to restore man's knowledge of eternal truth, including man's knowledge of his own nature, his relation to other persons, and his relation to God. Sophia Institute Press® serves this end in numerous ways: it publishes translations of foreign works to make them accessible to English-speaking readers; it brings out-of-print books back into print; and it publishes important new books that fulfill the ideals of Sophia Institute®. These books afford readers a rich source of the enduring wisdom of mankind.

Sophia Institute Press® makes these high-quality books available to the general public by using advanced technology and by soliciting donations to subsidize its general publishing costs. Your generosity can help Sophia Institute Press®

to provide the public with editions of works containing the enduring wisdom of the ages. Please send your tax-deductible contribution to the address below. We also welcome your questions, comments, and suggestions.

For your free catalog, call:
Toll-free: 1-800-888-9344

*or write:*
Sophia Institute Press®
Box 5284, Manchester, NH 03108

*or visit our website:*
www.sophiainstitute.com